Words in **bold** are explained in the Glossary on pages 30-31.

Minibeasts

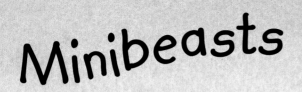

Worms tunnelling in soil, slithering snails and buzzing bees are all minibeasts. You can find minibeasts nearly everywhere – if you know where to look...

buddleia

rose

Spider

Ladybird

fox

Snail

Beetle

Woodlice

nettles

Ladybird

4

Large white
butterfly

Peacock
butterfly

sunflower

Tortoiseshell
butterfly

Bumblebee

foxglove

Woodlice

Slug

Centipede

PICTURE SEARCH

★ search for minibeasts crawling
on the ground
★ search for minibeasts flying
through the air

5

Minibeast families

Every minibeast belongs to a family. It looks like other members of its family in many ways. You can work out which family a minibeast belongs to if you look at it carefully.

Wasps

A wasp is an insect. All insects have 6 legs and a body with 3 parts, which is protected by a hard case.

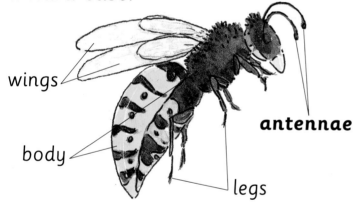

wings

body

antennae

legs

Slugs and snails

Slugs and snails have soft, moist bodies and 4 **tentacles**. Snails have shells on their backs.

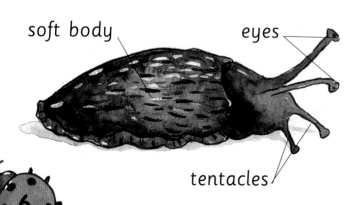

soft body

eyes

tentacles

Spiders

There are thousands of different kinds of spider but they all have 8 legs and a body with 2 parts.

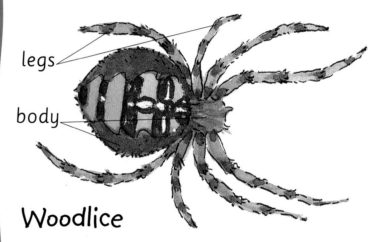

legs

body

Woodlice

Grey woodlice have 7 pairs of legs and 7 tough plates of armour to protect their bodies.

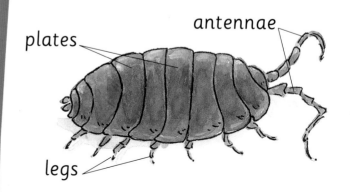

plates

antennae

legs

GO ON A MINIBEAST HUNT

Take a magnifying glass, a pencil and a notebook and go on a minibeast hunt. Be very quiet so you don't scare them away. Here are some places to look.

On leaves

Look for tiny **aphids** sucking juice from leaves and stems, and for ladybirds eating the aphids.

 WARNING: Don't touch minibeasts unless an adult is there to help you. Put back stones and leaves if you move them.

On flowers

Look for bees and butterflies on flowers drinking sweet juice called **nectar**.

Under stones

Slugs and snails dry out in the sun. Look for them under stones and in damp shady places.

In fallen leaves

Woodlice eat dead wood and plants. You can find them hidden under fallen leaves.

MAKE A MINIBEAST MAP

Draw a map of your garden or a park. Add pictures of minibeasts in the places where you spotted them. Name as many as you can.

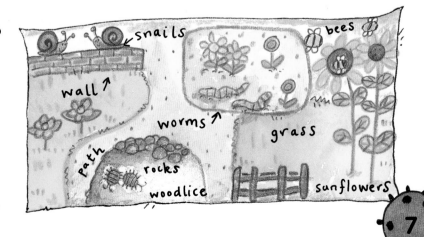

7

Fluttering butterflies

In the summer, butterflies struggle out of **pupas** and fly away on colourful wings. You can see them visiting flowers and resting on sunny walls.

buddleia

Red admiral

Painted lady

nasturtium

Large white butterfly

cabbage

Peacock butterfly

thyme

PICTURE SEARCH
* search for brown cases called pupas, where caterpillars turn into butterflies
* search for butterfly eggs hidden on the underside of the leaves

pupa

Small tortoiseshell butterfly

Adult butterfly hatching from pupa

Small tortoiseshell eggs

Red admiral eggs

nettles

Caterpillars hatching

Red admiral caterpillar

9

From egg to butterfly

Some creatures change shape as they grow.
When this happens it is called **metamorphosis**.

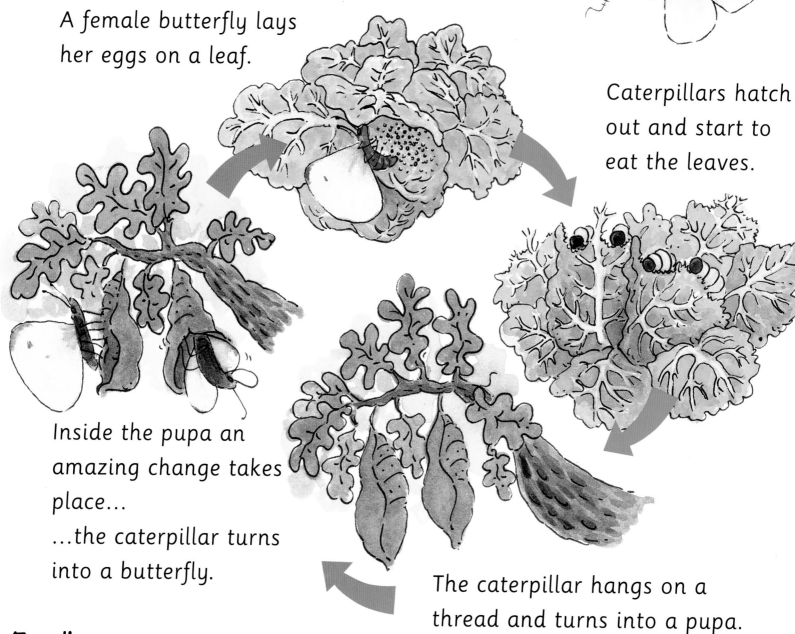

A female butterfly lays
her eggs on a leaf.

Caterpillars hatch
out and start to
eat the leaves.

Inside the pupa an
amazing change takes
place...
...the caterpillar turns
into a butterfly.

The caterpillar hangs on a
thread and turns into a pupa.

Feeding

Butterflies have long hollow tongues
like drinking straws, to suck up nectar from
deep inside flowers. When they
are not feeding, they curl
their tongues away.

hollow tongue

LOOK FOR BUTTERFLY COLOURS

butterfly

caterpillar

pupa

Green caterpillars and brown pupas are difficult to spot among leaves and twigs. Butterflies are often brightly coloured to help a male and female find each other. First, copy this picture of plants.

Now copy the butterfly, caterpillar and pupa and cut them out. Try putting them in different places on your picture. Where are they well hidden and where are they easy to spot?

TRY OUT A 'BUTTERFLY TONGUE'

Find a party blower that unrolls when you blow it – like a butterfly tongue. Place a plastic cup on its side for the inside of a flower. Try to hit the bottom of the cup with your 'butterfly tongue'.

toot!

Spinning spiders

Spiders spin silk and **weave** sticky webs to trap their food. In the early morning you can see webs covered in dew sparkling in the sunlight.

spinneret

silk thread

funnel web

Grass spider

Orb web spider

Harvestman Spider

Zebra spider

Water spider

Prey wrapped up in
a parcel of silk

PICTURE SEARCH

★ search for tiny baby spiders called
spiderlings just hatched from their eggs
★ search for the spiders that have been
busy spinning each different shaped web

hammock
web

Mesh web

Tiger
spider

8 eyes

Veil web
spider

Crab
spider

fangs

Spiderlings

Wolf spider

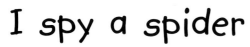

I spy a spider

Look for spiders hiding in
cracks and dark places
in the garden shed.

Spinnerets

A spider makes silk to weave and
mend its sticky web. The silk is
squeezed into threads with
spinnerets in the end of its body.

spinneret

silk thread

Prey wrapped up in
a parcel of silk

Got you!

When its **prey** gets trapped in
the web, the spider wraps it
up in silk so it
can't escape.

Fangs

The spider bites its captured prey
with **fangs** that look like teeth. It
injects it with **poison** and carries
it off to eat later.

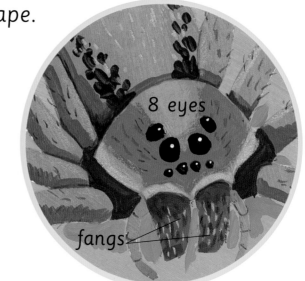

8 eyes

fangs

LYING IN WAIT

Some spiders lie in wait with one leg touching a line of silk attached to their web. When they feel the line move, they rush out to catch their prey. Lightly blow on a spider's web. Does a spider rush out?

BE A SPIDER

Tie cotton between two chairs – stretch it tightly. Put a finger on the cotton and shut your eyes. Ask a friend to tap the cotton lightly. When you feel the cotton move, try to catch your friend's hand.

SPIDERS IN THE BATH

Look for a spider inside your house. Keep a diary of when it comes out and when it hides away.

15

Slithering slugs and snails

Slugs and snails have soft, slimy bodies. Snails also have curly **shells**. They hide in dark, damp places and come out at night and in the rain.

tentacle

Field slug

slime trail

Field slugs

potato

Banded snail

Ramshorn snail

Pond snail

PICTURE SEARCH

★ search for slugs and snails
★ spot things that are the same about a snail and a slug
★ spot things that are different

shell

Banded snail

foot

Keel slug

Leopard slug

eggs

17

Moving and hiding

Slugs and snails dry out in the sunshine, so they come out on damp, rainy days.

Slithering

Slugs and snails ripple their bodies to move along. They make slime to help them slither over the ground and climb walls. They leave a trail of slime behind.

slime trail

Shells

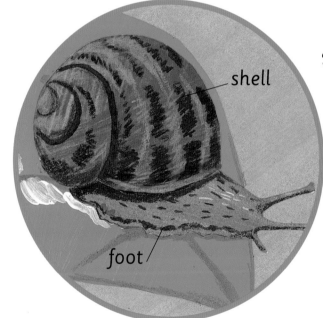

shell

foot

When a snail is in danger, it pulls its body right inside its shell. In dry weather, it can make a sticky door for its shell and shut itself in.

Tentacles

Slugs and snails have 2 pairs of tentacles with eyes on the end of the longest pair to see and feel all around them.

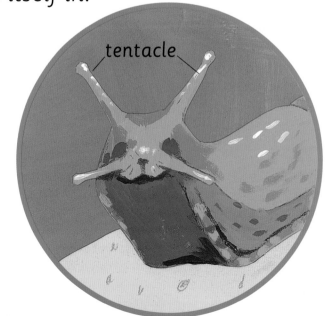

tentacle

BIG FOOT

Slugs and snails are gastropods, which means 'stomach foot'. Put a snail on a clear plastic food tray. Turn it upside down – it won't fall off! Watch how it ripples its body to move along on its 'foot'.

Try putting a blob of flour and water paste next to the snail. Look through the underside of the tray and watch it eat.

HOW DOES A SNAIL EAT?

A snail's tongue is covered with thousands of tiny teeth. Find a snail eating a leaf and listen – you might hear a scraping sound as it rubs the leaf with its rough tongue.

SPARKLING SLIME

Let the snail slither across a piece of dark card. It will leave behind a lovely glistening trail.

 WARNING: Put the snail back in a damp place!

Tunnellers and diggers

Hidden away on the woodland floor, minibeasts are busy digging in the earth and munching dead logs and leaves.

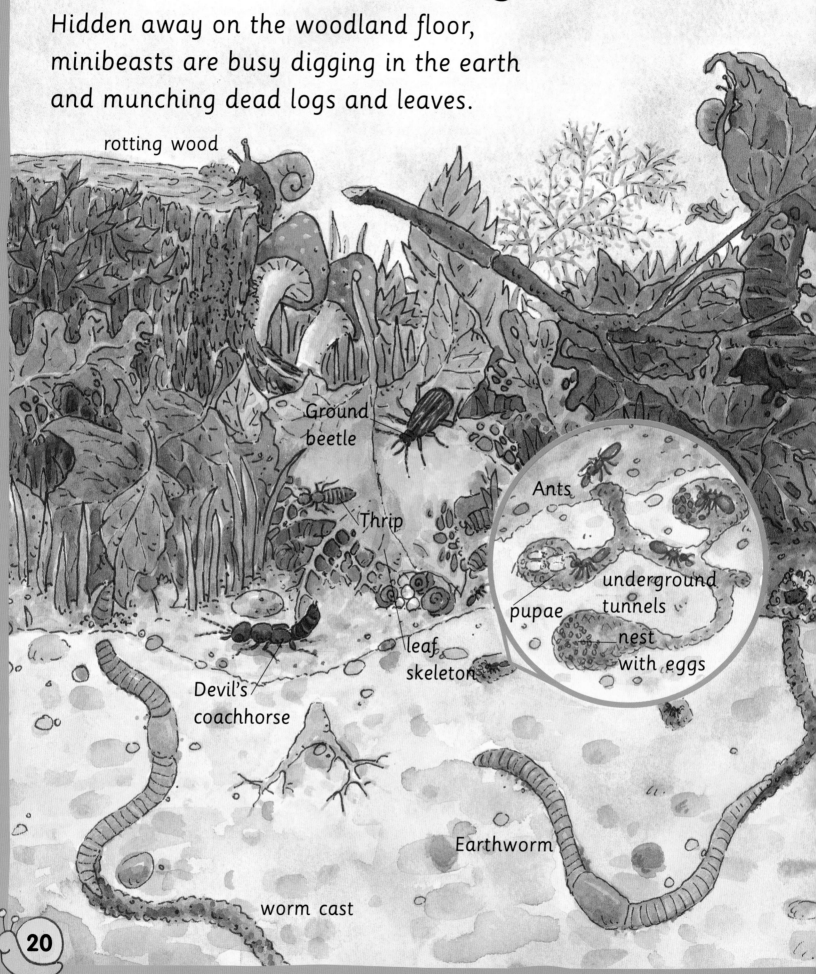

rotting wood

Ground beetle

Thrip

Ants

pupae

underground tunnels

nest with eggs

leaf skeleton

Devil's coachhorse

Earthworm

worm cast

PICTURE SEARCH
* search for minibeasts that are the same colour as earth and wood
* search for minibeasts that are the same colour as stones

Tiger beetle

Green tiger beetle

rotting wood

Pill bug
Woodlouse

Centipede

Stag beetle

Millipede

Decomposers

Can you see minibeasts chewing and tunnelling through this log? They help to break up or **decompose** dead wood and plants and make new, rich soil.

Ants

Ants tunnel in the earth to make their nests. They carry insects and seeds underground to feed the queen ant and her tiny ant **grubs**.

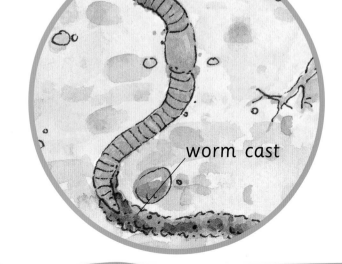

Ants

pupae

nest with eggs

underground tunnels

Woodlice

Woodlice eat dead wood and plants. A type of woodlouse called a pill bug, can curl up in a ball when it is in danger.

Woodlice

Pill bug

Worms

Worms eat soil as they tunnel their way through the ground. Soil passes through them and comes out at the other end, leaving a **worm cast**.

worm cast

MAKE A WORMERY

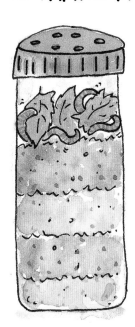

Ask an adult to make holes in the lid of a clean, clear plastic sweet jar. Fill 2/3rds of the jar with layers of damp soil and put leaves on top.

Carefully add 2 or 3 worms from the garden and put the jar in a dark place.

After a while, see how the worms have made tunnels and pulled the leaves into the soil.

LOOK FOR ANT TRAILS

Ants like sweet, sugary food. Soak crumbs of bread in sugar mixed with water and put them around the garden or yard. The ants will carry the sugary bread back to their nest in a line. Follow the lines and you will find the ants' nest.

WHISPERING WORMS

Put a large worm on a piece of paper on a table and lay your head next to it. Keep very quiet and you might hear the tiny bristles on the worm's skin brushing the paper as it moves along.

WARNING: Put the worms back in the soil!

Bees and wasps

Bees drink sweet nectar from flowers and wasps eat fruit. In the summer, wasps buzz around sugary food like jam and soft drinks.

swarm of honeybees

honey

Honeybee

pollen dust

pollen pouch

eye

tube for sucking nectar

antenna

Honeybee

wasp nest

honeybee nest

antennae

Wasp

wings

PICTURE SEARCH
★ spot the things that are the same about a bee and a wasp
★ spot the things that are different

Bumblebee

pollen

The story of honey

Honey bees carry nectar back to their nests. They eat some of it and use the rest to make honey to eat later.

Honeycomb

In the nest, bees make a honeycomb with wax. Honey and pollen are stored inside some cells and others are full of eggs and growing grubs.

stores of honey

grubs

Pollen

Flowers make yellow dust called pollen. When a bee visits a flower it gets covered in pollen, it combs the pollen into pouches on its legs.

pollen pouch

 WARNING: Bees and wasps can give you a painful sting.

Wasps

Common wasps make paper to build their nests by chewing up little bits of wood. The queen wasp lays an egg in each papery cell.

DO A WAGGLE DANCE

Bees do a waggle dance to show other bees where to find food.

Hide an apple and make up a waggle dance to show your friends where it is. How fast can they find it?

SMELLS AND COLOURS

Flowers have bright colours and scents to attract insects. Some flowers have a pattern of spots and lines called a honey guide that leads the visitor to the nectar.

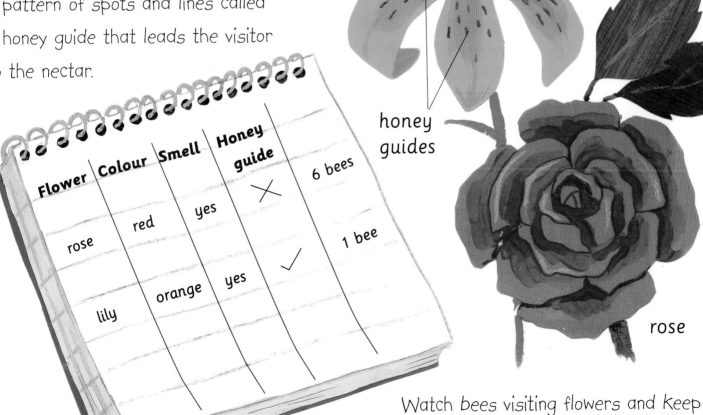

lily

honey guides

rose

Flower	Colour	Smell	Honey guide	
rose	red	yes	✕	6 bees
lily	orange	yes	✓	1 bee

Watch bees visiting flowers and keep a record like this one of what you see.

More minibeasts

Ladybirds

A 7 spot ladybird is a little beetle with 7 black spots on its bright red wing cases. Gardeners like them because they eat garden pests called aphids.

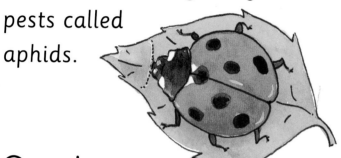

Grasshoppers

Grasshoppers rub their legs and wings together to make a chirping sound. They have very long back legs for leaping through the grass.

Earwigs

Earwigs look fierce, but they are not hunters. They come out in groups at night to feed on fruit and flowers.

Centipedes

'Centipede' means a hundred feet – but a centipede can have between 34 and 354 legs. It hides in dark places in the day and comes out at night to hunt for food.

Dragonflies

A dragonfly starts life underwater as a brown nymph. After a year or so, it climbs out of the water and changes into a dragonfly and flies away on see-through wings.

Stag beetles

Stag beetles have tough brown wing cases. The males have big **antler**-shaped jaws which they use for fighting each other.

BE A MINIBEAST SPOTTER

★ Be patient – if you're very quiet and still, you won't frighten minibeasts away.

★ Use your ears – listen for buzzing, chirping and rustling sounds that tell you a minibeast is nearby.

★ Use your eyes – turn to page 7 to find out where to look for minibeasts.

Be careful

★ try not to disturb minibeasts. If you lift a stone, always put it back in place.

★ watch out for minibeasts that sting.

You need

★ a magnifying glass to help you see the minibeasts more clearly.

★ a notebook and coloured pencils to make a note of what you spot.

Glossary

Antennae

Antennae or 'feelers' are the stalks on a minibeast's head. They pick up what is going on all around the minibeast and help it to find food and keep it safe.

Antlers

Male deer are called stags. They have horns called antlers, which are shaped like branches. Stag beetles get their name from deer because the males have enormous jaws which look like antlers.

Aphids

Aphids are tiny bugs that damage plants by sucking sticky juice from their stems.

Decompose

To decompose means to break down. When plants die, they decompose or break down and become part of the soil.

Fangs

Fangs are big sharp teeth. Spiders have two fangs, which they use to grab and poison any small animals that they catch in their webs.

Grubs

Grubs are the babies that hatch from insect's eggs. They look different from the adults that they become.

Metamorphosis

Metamorphosis is the name for what happens when a creature changes shape as it grows. A butterfly for example changes from a caterpillar to a butterfly.

Nectar

Nectar is a sweet sugary liquid made by flowers. It attracts insects to visit the flowers to feed.

Poison

A poison is something that can either harm or kill animals or plants. Spiders poison animals that get caught in their webs.

Pollen

Pollen is the yellow powder made by flowers. Bees collect pollen and carry it back to their hives for food.

Prey

Prey are animals that other animals hunt for food. Spiders make webs to trap their prey.

Pupa

A caterpillar makes a hard case around itself to protect it while it turns into a butterfly. When it is wrapped in this case, it is called a pupa. A pupa is also called a chrysalis.

Spinnerets

A spider has spinnerets at the end of its body. It uses them to squeeze the silk it makes into threads and to make its web.

Tentacles

Snails and slugs have four tentacles on their heads. Two of the tentacles have eyes on the ends. The snails or slugs wave the tentacles about to see, feel and smell what is going on around them.

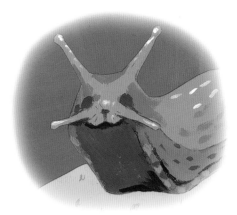

Weave

Cloth is made by weaving threads in and out of each other. We say that spiders weave their webs with threads of silk.

Worm cast

A worm cast is a curly shape of tiny bits of soil that a worm leaves behind as it munches through the earth.

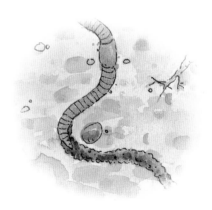

Index

32